THE G.I. SERIES

Grunts
U.S. Infantry in Vietnam

Private First Class George J. Pigmtora holds a first aid dressing to his chest after being wounded during Operation Masher in January 1965. Pigmtora is wearing the OG107 utility shirt, with gold and black U.S. Army tape, common at this early stage of the war. The private has tied strips of burlap to his helmet to break up its outline. The bandage he is holding to hi chest was carried by every infantryman as part of his load bearing equipment and was meant to provide emergency first aid until more advanced care could be provided.

THE G.I. SERIES

THE ILLUSTRATED HISTORY OF THE AMERICAN SOLDIER, HIS UNIFORM AND HIS EQUIPMENT

Grunts
U.S. Infantry in Vietnam

Christopher J. Anderson

Greenhill Books
LONDON

Stackpole Books
PENNSYLVANIA

Greenhill Books

Grunts: U.S. Infantry in Vietnam first published 1998 by
Greenhill Books, Lionel Leventhal Limited, Park House,
1 Russell Gardens, London NW11 9NN
and
Stackpole Books, 5067 Ritter Road, Mechanicsburg,
PA 17055, USA

British Library Cataloguing in Publication Data
Anderson, Christopher J.
Grunts: U.S. Infantry in Vietnam. - (The G.I. Series: the illus-
trated history of the American soldier, his uniform and his
equipment; v.13)
1. United States. Army. Infantry - History 2. Vietnamese Conflict, 1961–1975
I. Title
356.1'0973'0904

ISBN 1-85367-326-9

Library of Congress Cataloging-in-Publication Data
Anderson, Christopher J.
Grunts: U.S. Infantry in Vietnam / by Christopher J. Anderson.
    p.   cm. — (G.I. Series: 13)
ISBN 1-85367-326-9
1. United States. Army—Infantry—History—20th century.
2. United States. Army—Uniforms—History—20th century.
3. United States. Army—Equipment—History—20th century.
4. Vietnamese Conflict. 1961–1975—Equipment and supplies. I. Title. II. Series.
UD373.A53 1998
356'.11'0973—dc21   98-18239
                                                         CIP

DEDICATION

To all veterans of America's longest war, and to my father
who nurtured in me a love of books.

The photographs in this book are from the U.S. National
Archives

Designed by DAG Publications Ltd
Designed by David Gibbons
Layout by Anthony A. Evans
Printed in Hong Kong

Some of the photographs in this book were
taken under wartime conditions. Some are not of
the highest quality, and are included because of
their extreme rarity.

GRUNTS:
U.S. INFANTRY IN VIETNAM

While American advisors had been present in the Republic of Vietnam since the 1950s, the first significant commitment of U.S. forces to Vietnam began in 1965 after President Lyndon Johnson approved offensive operations there by American ground forces. By the end of that year, 184,000 American soldiers were fully engaged in the ground war in Vietnam.

Over the course of the next seven years, the United States and its allies would employ their full economic, industrial and technological might in an unsuccessful attempt to defeat the forces of the Communist North Vietnamese. During the ground war, the United States used a huge assortment of advanced technology to destroy enemy forces. Despite all of this technology, the war in Vietnam was essentially an infantryman's war fought as thousands of small unit actions. For all of the dramatic images of waves of helicopters and B-52 bombers sweeping down on the enemy, the most typical scene of the Vietnam War is that of a squad or platoon of overburdened infantrymen struggling through the jungle or along a rice paddy.

The infantryman in Vietnam knew that no matter how many bombing missions, artillery bombardments, and helicopter assaults were used to assault the enemy, in the end, it would be a squad of infantrymen who would have to locate and destroy the enemy soldiers waiting in the jungle.

The 'upclose' nature of the war bred a great deal of pride in the 11Bs, the Army's occupational code for infantrymen, who began to call themselves 'grunts' as a slang term taken from the sound they made as they struggled under the weight of packs and equipment. 'Grunt' has become one of the most evocative terms of the war and is still used today to refer to an infantry soldier.

The soldiers who arrived in Vietnam in 1965 were just a trickle of what would become an eventual flood of American personnel. The first troops to Vietnam were all highly trained soldiers of a peacetime army. An infantryman in 1965 would have arrived in Vietnam wearing an OG107 utility uniform. The utility, or fatigue, uniform was made of a heavy duty cotton sateen material. The full uniform consisted of hat, shirt, trousers and service boots. The visored utility hat resembled a baseball cap, and had stiffening added to the front so that either rank insignia or a unit crest could be pinned to it. Many soldiers preferred to acquire private purchase copies of the utility hat as these tended to look more stylish than the issue variety. Utility hats were never well received by the individual enlisted soldier, but continued to be worn throughout the war.

The fatigue shirt, worn over a white cotton t-shirt, was closed with plastic buttons and featured two patch pockets sewn to the chest. The first pattern of utility shirt can be distinguished by the squared flaps on the chest pockets, later models of utility shirt having clipped corner pockets. Until 1966, the utility shirt was adorned with a white name tape on the right breast, black and gold U.S. Army tape on the left breast, full color unit insignia on the left shoulder and green and gold rank insignia on the sleeves. After 1966, the insignia began to be worn in a 'subdued' black and olive drab configuration.

The utility trousers had two patch pockets at the thighs and two on the hips. The trousers were held in place with a black web belt with brass roller buckle. The trouser legs were then bloused into the black leather service boot. This boot was a high top, lace up boot, patterned after the paratrooper boot of World War II.

As the American commitment in Vietnam continued to grow, efforts were made to improve the clothing that was being worn by soldiers in the field. The tropical combat uniform that began to be introduced in 1963 was a vast improvement over the utility uniform. The uniform consisted of a utility cap, shirt, trousers and jungle boots and was constructed of lightweight cotton poplin. The utility uniform would eventually be issued in three different patterns.

The jacket was worn bloused over the trousers. It had four bellows pockets, shoulder epaulets, side adjustment tabs and a gas flap. A distinctive feature of the first model uniform was the exposed buttons on the pockets. The second pattern jacket was similar but, the buttons on the pockets were concealed after it was discovered that the exposed buttons became caught on equipment and other obstructions. The second pattern jacket also did away with the gas flap because most soldiers in the field simply cut this extra piece of fabric out of the jackets. The third and final pattern of jacket also had concealed buttons, but designers had removed the shoulder epaulets and side adjustment tabs. Another distinctive feature of the third pattern utility jacket was that it was constructed in rip stop cotton. Rip stop cotton was woven from standard cotton poplin with a grid of nylon thread woven in. Rip stop material can be identified by the grid like pattern visible in the material. All three pattern jackets can be found with the full color and subdued insignia attached. When in the field, the jackets were quite often worn with no insignia at all.

Although intended to be worn underneath the fatigue jacket, the issue olive drab t-shirt was often worn, frequently with the sleeves removed, as an outer garment.

Like the jacket, the trousers were also inspired by the World War II airborne uniform. The first pattern trousers were made of cotton poplin and featured two large bellows pockets on the hip and a draw string at the bottom. The second pattern was similar to the first, but it had concealed buttons and was made of rip stop cotton like the third pattern jacket. The trousers were worn with the black web belt with brass buckle.

When the new utility uniform was first introduced it was worn with the baseball cap that had been a part of the earlier OG107 uniform. This remained the case until 1968 when the cotton tropical combat 'boonie' hat with a wide brim and foliage loops began to reach units in the field. However, as more and more soldiers who were products of the draft and civilian society began to arrive in Vietnam, the chief attraction of the hat was that it could be individualised by men in the field. 'Boonie' hats are found in period pictures being worn in hundreds of different configurations and many surviving examples are found adorned with a variety of pins, badges and embroidery.

While the 'boonie' hat was immensely popular with the soldiers who wore it, it was loathed by many of the higher ranking officers in Vietnam. Lieutenant General Creighton Abrahms, who followed Lieutenant General William Westmoreland as commander of ground forces in Vietnam, tried to have it banned. Despite his best efforts, the 'boonie' hat survived the disapproval of higher headquarters and was worn until the end of the war.

The third pattern jungle fatigue uniform and 'boonie' hat were manufactured in ERDL camouflage pattern, although this was not frequently seen on infantrymen in Vietnam. The limited supply of these camouflaged uniforms generally restricted their use to special forces and reconnaissance units.

Another very successful component of the jungle uniform was the nylon and leather jungle boot. These boots were found to be lighter in weight and easier to dry than the black leather service boot. During the course of the war they were issued in a number of patterns. Earlier boots featured a vibram sole, and later patterns featured a panama sole that did not become clogged with mud as easily. These boots also came with a steel plate inserted into the sole to guard against booby traps.

The highly functional tropical combat uniform was a vast improvement over the earlier uniform and proved to be popular with the G.I.s in Vietnam, becoming the predominantly used uniform of the war. It should be noted that due to initial shortages of these uniforms, the 'jungle' uniform was issued to troops only after their arrival in Vietnam and were turned in prior to their departure from the country. The development and use of the jungle fatigue uniform was one of the great success stories of the conflict and set the stage for American military uniforms worn to this day.

All of a grunt's equipment was worn over the fatigue uniform. The infantryman carried his combat load with the various components of the M1956 load bearing equipment (LBE). This canvas equipment featured individual components attached to a pistol belt. The G.I. could attach two ammunition pouches that would carry spare magazines for the M-14 and later the M-16 rifle, canteen, first aid or compass, entrenching tool and combat field 'butt' pack. The belt was supported by attached suspenders.

In 1967 the Army began to switch over to nylon components of the M1956 gear. This nylon gear was superior to the earlier canvas material, but was never received in sufficient quantities to be issued in sets. Instead, individual components were mixed with the earlier canvas equipment.

Not long after his arrival 'in country' a soldier would begin to make modifications to his equipment to increase practicality and comfort. After 1966, one of the first things that a grunt would do would be to discard the 'butt' pack of the M1956 gear in favor of the lightweight rucksack. The typical infantry operation would require soldiers to spend prolonged periods in the field unsupported from the outside. This would require an infantry patrol to carry all of its needs on its back. The 'butt' pack was too small to carry everything. The lightweight rucksack consisted of a nylon bag attached to a tubular steel frame. To the frame of the rucksack, grunts would have attached extra canteens and ammunition or any other equipment needed on a long operation.

In a further attempt to lighten his load, many infantrymen discarded the load bearing equipment entirely in favor of bandoliers worn as belts around the body.

In an effort to provide some ballistic protection, armored 'flak' jackets were available to infantrymen in Vietnam. The most common vest was the M1952 armored vest. This vest consisted of layers of nylon sewn into a green nylon shell, closed by a front zipper. Later, the improved M69 armored vest was introduced which, unlike the earlier M1952 vest, featured a short collar to improve protection for the neck. Both of these vests were worn at the same time during the war. Despite the added protection that the vests offered, they were frequently not worn by infantrymen. Many grunts preferred to take their chances without the body armor rather than carry an additional eight pounds on jungle patrols.

While body armor was frequently discarded, the M1 helmet was always worn on operations. The M1 helmet worn in Vietnam was unchanged from the helmet worn during World War II. Over the helmet was worn the reversible leaf pattern helmet cover. This helmet cover had a green predominant leaf pattern on one side, and a brown predominant pattern on the other. In Vietnam the green shade was often worn outside. Frequently soldiers would pen graffiti on their helmet covers to add a touch of individuality. This sort of adornment on the helmet and elsewhere began to be much more prevalent as the new recruits arriving in Vietnam began to display many of the anti-war sentiments being expressed at home in America. To secure the cover on the helmet shell, an elasticated helmet band was worn over the cover. Although originally intended to secure foliage to the outside of the helmet, the band was usually used as a place to secure insect repellant, gun oil or spare cigarettes. The elasticated band was also used to secure pins or other decorations at the soldier's discretion.

Along with the burden of his equipment and helmet, the soldier could have carried a variety of weapons. Until 1965 the standard rifle of the grunt was the M-14 rifle, a more refined version of the M1 Garand that had been used during World War II and Korea. It was a 7.62mm magazine fed, selective fire weapon and could be fired at either semi- or full-automatic.

In 1965 the M-16 began to replace the M-14 as the infantryman's standard rifle. The M-16 was revolutionary for its time, its lightweight plastic and stamped metal construction making it lighter than any previous American weapon. It could fire its 5.56mm rounds at either semi- or full-automatic. The lighter weight of the weapon and the weapons ammunition made it ideal for the jungles of Vietnam.

Additional fire power was provided to an infantry squad by the M-60 General Purpose Machine Gun (GPMG), the standard squad automatic weapon of the Vietnam era. The M-60 had a high (550 rounds per minute) rate of fire, and so most members of an infantry squad would carry additional ammunition for the squad's M-60. The weapon itself was usually carried over the shoulder by the gunner.

For indirect fire, the M79 'thumper' grenade launcher was very effective. This weapon, resembling a sawn off shotgun, could fire 40mm grenade rounds at enemy positions. In addition to the M79's grenades, each squad member would have carried several M26 fragmentation grenades. These grenades could be carried attached to the M1956 ammunition pouches. The M18A1 claymore mine was carried by grunts for use in ambushes or in defense of static positions.

The M-60 machine gun, M79 grenade launcher, M-14 and M-16 rifles were the most frequently used infantry weapons of the war. However, the typical American squad could also call on a number of other support weapons ranging from 81mm mortar rounds to F4 Phantom air strikes if the situation warranted it.

Fully uniformed and equipped, the grunt of Vietnam would have conducted most of his operations as a member of a ten-man rifle squad. The rifle squad was the building block of all infantry formations in Vietnam. Three rifle squads, a platoon headquarters of three men and a weapons squad of 11 men made up a platoon. Three platoons, a weapons platoon and a headquarters would make up a company. Although there were larger organisations, the ground war in Vietnam was largely fought at the company level and below.

However, during larger operations, such as Operation Junction City in 1967, the Tet Offensive in 1968 and Operation Russell Beach in 1969, larger formations such as brigades and divisions did see action. During the war the army deployed nine divisions and numerous brigades. Although deployed as divisions, these larger units had little relevancy and an infantry soldier's first loyalty was to his company, regiment and fellow grunts.

Much has been said about the many problems that the army suffered during the Vietnam war, however the uniforms and equipment that were developed by the army in response to the harsh conditions encountered by the infantry soldiers during that war were, by and large, a great success. More than 25 years since the end of the war, much of the equipment developed for the war in Vietnam is still in use, or has inspired equipment currently in use. It should also be remembered that the infantry soldiers of the U.S. Army were consistently able to defeat the very best that the North Vietnamese had.

FOR FURTHER READING

Summers, Jr., Harry G., *Historical Atlas of the Vietnam War,* Houghton Mifflin, 1995
Thompson, Leroy, *The U.S. Army in Vietnam,* David & Charles, 1990
Stanton, Shelby, *The Rise and Fall of an American Army*, Presidio, 1990
Stanton, Shelby, *U.S. Army Uniforms of the Vietnam War*, Stackpole Books, 1989
Lyles, Kevin, *Vietnam Uniforms in Color Photographs*, Windrow & Green Ltd, 1994
Lyles, Kevin, *U.S. Infantry in Vietnam*, Concord Publications, 1996

Above: A soldier takes a break while on patrol. He has folded up the brim of his jungle hat; soldiers in Vietnam would routinely personalise these hats, earning them the disdain of higher command that had been reserved for the beanie hat in World War II. This soldier is carrying extra ammunition in a cotton bandolier which could carry seven spare magazines for the M-16 rifle.

Left: A radioman calls in his position during a patrol. He has attached his AN/PRC 10 radio to the back of a lightweight rucksack. He has also attached several plastic canteens that have been removed from their canvas carriers. In his right hand he carries the M79 'thumper' grenade launcher.

Above: A group of infantrymen confer after arriving on a Landing Zone (LZ). The soldiers in the picture are wearing the third pattern jungle fatigues. As was common practice during operations in the field, these fatigues do not have insignia sewn to them. The men are also travelling light and have attached very little to their M1956 web equipment.

Right: During an operation in 1966, soldiers secure the perimeter of their LZ as the Huey helicopter that delivered them takes off. The soldier in the foreground has an M203 grenade launcher attached to his M-16 rifle. He has also draped spare ammunition for his squad's M-60 machine gun around his chest. The M-60 had such a terrific rate of fire that on operations all of the men in a squad would carry extra ammunition for the gun.

Above: Soldiers of the 1st Infantry Division arrive in Vietnam by landing craft. These men are new to Vietnam and are still wearing the standard OG107 cotton utility uniform. The OG107s were worn in Vietnam until sufficient supplies of jungle fatigues had arrived. These men also wear a combination of steel helmets and OD utility caps.

Left: Soldiers of the 9th Infantry Division prepare for an operation in the Mekong Delta region. The soldier standing at left has draped a couple of bandoliers over his flak jacket. While it gave extra protection, the flak jacket also added weight and increased body temperature. To make themselves more comfortable, some of these men are not wearing the fatigue jacket under their flak armor.

Top left: These men carry a wounded comrade out of the jungle on a poncho for evacuation. The man at the front of the litter party carries ammunition for his M-16 in a cotton bandolier that he wears over his standard M1956 equipment. He has slipped a packet of matches into the camouflage band of his helmet to keep them dry. The soldier with his back to the camera illustrates the appearance of the lightweight rucksack when full. A common practice during lengthy operations was the attachment of additional canteens to soldiers' packs.

Lower left: An M113 armored personnel carrier takes up its position. While armored vehicles did not play as prominent a role in Vietnam as they had done in earlier wars, armored vehicles were used during the Vietnam war to clear highways and protect convoys. The M113 could transport infantrymen to the battlefield or, with the addition of a .50 caliber machine gun as pictured here, could be used as an armored assault vehicle.

Above: On 31 January 1967, two soldiers search for the enemy with a 'people sniffer': an electronic device designed to locate hidden enemy personnel.

Right: A soldier prepares to clear an enemy position with a flame thrower. Due to their weight and the vulnerable position in which they placed their users, flame throwers would not generally have been carried on a patrol or operation, but would have been brought up to infantrymen who had found an enemy bunker or tunnel position.

Top left: Officers establish their command post (CP) within a secure landing zone (LZ). They are all wearing the jungle fatigue uniform. The man holding the map, on the right, is wearing the second model of jungle fatigues, identified by the epaulets on the jacket. The two men working the radio, on the left of the picture, are wearing just the pistol belt with no other gear. They have secured their radio to a packboard that they are supporting with a stick.

Lower left: Two American soldiers search a Vietnamese home for signs of Viet Cong guerrillas. The soldier on the left is carrying all of his immediate needs in the thigh pockets of his jungle fatigue pants.

Top right: A medic prepares his aid station beside an M113 armored personnel carrier. The medic is wearing the third pattern jungle jacket with concealed buttons and the issue olive green t-shirt underneath the jacket. This was unusual in the heat of Vietnam. He has no insignia or patches on his jacket. He carries his medical supplies in discarded wooden ammunition crates. On extended operations he would carry all of his equipment in specially designed medics' bags.

Lower right: Lieutenant Colonel Horne inspects a private's M-16 rifle prior to shipping out for Vietnam. Both men wear the OG107 utilities that would have been worn until arrival in Vietnam. Horne wears a .45 caliber pistol in a black leather shoulder holster worn across his chest. He wears subdued branch of service insignia on the collar of his first pattern utility jacket. The first pattern jacket did not have button cuffs. The private being inspected wears a newly issued set of second pattern utilities with rounded pocket flaps and buttoned cuffs.

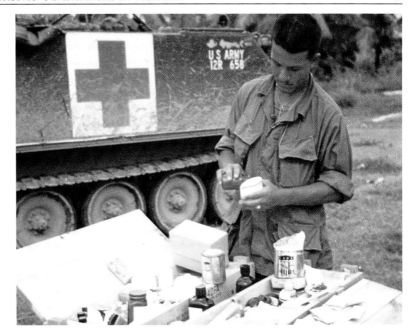

Medal of Honor recipient, Specialist Clarence E. Sasser, has his official portrait taken in March 1969. Specialist Sasser is wearing the green service uniform with khaki shirt and black tie. On his left shoulder Sasser wears the patch of the 9th Infantry Division. In addition to the Medal of Honor that he wears around his neck, Sasser wears ribbons for (first row, left to right) the Distinguished Service Cross and the Purple Heart, and (second row, left to right) the National Defense Service Medal and the Republic of Vietnam Service Medal. Above his ribbons Sasser wears the Combat Medics Badge. Note also the Expert Marksman's badge, pinned to his pocket flap. Suspended from this badge by the small loops would usually be a 'Q-bar' identifying the type of weapon with which the wearer achieved this proficiency rating. Sasser was awarded the medal for actions in January 1968.

Right: Soldiers off-load from a UH-1 Huey. This photograph is probably staged as the two men at the front have creases in their trousers. However, everything being worn by these men is typical of the uniform worn by the infantry in Vietnam early in the war. All of the men in the picture are wearing the OG107 cotton sateen utility uniform and black leather combat boots. Underneath their utility uniform they wear the white cotton t-shirt.

Above: Lieutenant John Libs of the 16th Infantry Regiment, 1st Infantry Division, directs his platoon in October 1965. Libs is armed with an M-14 rifle, the primary infantry weapon of the G.I. early in the Vietnam war. It was the successor of the M1 Garand of World War II fame and could fire in either automatic or semi-automatic mode. Magazines containing 20 rounds for the rifle were carried in the front pouches of the M1956 web gear.

Left: A column of grunts advance during Operation Masher in January 1965. All of the men wear the OG107 utility uniform. The entire patrol has also added burlap to their helmets. The soldier kneeling second from the left is carrying three M72 Light Assault Anti-Tank Weapons (LAAW). While grunts rarely encountered enemy armor in Vietnam, the LAAWs were very effective portable artillery that could be used against heavily entrenched Viet Cong or North Vietnamese Army positions.

Lower left: Members of the 27th Infantry Regiment, 25th Infantry Division, use a scout dog to alert them to concealed enemy positions in September 1966. Both men are wearing the second pattern jungle utilities. The second pattern utilities can be distinguished by the concealed buttons and shoulder epaulets on the jackets. Sergeant Herald Fryer, standing on the left, has an olive and black subdued 25th Division patch on his left shoulder.

Right: An M-60 gunner waits for the enemy. He is wearing the first pattern OG107 utility jacket. Although he does not wear insignia on his jacket, his identity as a member of an airborne unit is revealed by the airborne chin strap on his helmet.

Opposite page, top: During Operation Cedar Falls in January 1967, Specialist Ronald Headly of the 25th Infantry Division checks on an enemy tunnel. Headly wears the second pattern OG107 utility shirt with clipped corner pockets. Interestingly, he is wearing subdued rank insignia on his right sleeve in addition to a non-subdued name tape, which was not common. He has also removed the camouflaged helmet cover from his helmet.

Opposite page, bottom: Members of the 5th Mechanized Infantry Division clear a VC trench in January 1967. The men are wearing a combination of OG107 utilities and first and second pattern jungle fatigues. Also of interest is the white t-shirt being worn by the man at the rear of the column. A variety of weapons are also being carried including two M79 grenade launchers, M-14 and M-16 rifles. The flashlight is a TL-122, a World War II design which is still in use to this day. Note also the standard issue M1911 A1 .45 caliber pistol.

Above: Private First Class George Nagel tries some field repairs using a sewing machine found in a VC tunnel. Private Nagel is wearing the second pattern jungle jacket with shoulder loops. He has rested his M79 grenade launcher against an olive green towel draped over his leg. Towels were often worn around the neck and used to wipe sweat from the face and head of soldiers.

Right: A soldier helps a comrade out of a Viet Cong tunnel complex. The soldier kneeling outside the hole wears the M1952 body armor vest over an olive green t-shirt. He has attached a smoke grenade that can be used to signal friendly forces.

Above: Private James Laurie uses a Sylvania battery powered 'sun gun' to search an enemy occupied cave in 1967. Private Laurie has wrapped an olive green towel around his neck to help with moisture. Specialty items such as the 'sun gun' were not commonly carried on operations, but were brought forward on an 'as needed' basis.

Below: Specialist Carl Thomas of the 1st Infantry Division prepares a claymore mine for demolition at the 1st Infantry Division's combat indoctrination course. The photograph provides a good illustration of the helmet cover worn on virtually all helmets during the Vietnam war. The helmet cover consisted of a leaf pattern camouflage with green predominating on one side and brown on the other. In Vietnam it was more common to see the green side worn on the outside.

Right: A member of the 9th Infantry Division eats his C-rations in his platoon's night camp. The soldier has attached a jackknife and P-38 can opener to his lightweight rucksack with the pull ring from a grenade. The Winston cigarettes are privately acquired; C-ration cigarettes came in packs of 10, not 20 as shown here. Also at the soldier's feet is a bottle of sauce. Ketchup or tabasco sauce was carried by many grunts in order to make the C-rations more palatable.

Above: Infantrymen of the 11th Armored Cavalry Regiment 'The Black Horse', move up on the enemy with the assistance of their M113 Armored Cavalry Assault Vehicles (ACAV). In this variant the M113 had an armored cupola and additional machine gun mounts on the upper hull. The man standing in the center has a camera draped around his neck and a movie camera in his left hand. Just visible on his left shoulder is a subdued patch of the Military Assistance Command Vietnam (MACV). This, and his military rank badge worn underneath the MACV patch, indicate that this man is an 'official' Army photographer.

Left: Colonel Miles leads members of the 39th Infantry Regiment out of the jungle after Operation Colby. He has sewn a subdued rank insignia to the front of his helmet. With the exception of the insignia on his helmet, there is nothing to distinguish the Colonel from the rest of his men. He has attached a smoke grenade to his unbuckled load bearing equipment. Also of interest is the World War II era fragmentation grenade that is attached to the right shoulder of his equipment harness.

Above: The grunts' standard rifle for the majority of the Vietnam conflict was the M-16 A1 rifle, pictured here with spare magazines and cleaning equipment. Developed to overcome the teething problems which plagued the M-16, the M-16 A1 is identifiable by its 'birdcage' muzzle brake and the forward assist device on the right side of the receiver. Also, the curved, 30-round magazine was a late addition which saw very little use, if any, during the Vietnam War.

Right: A 9th Infantry Division helicopter comes into an LZ to evacuate wounded soldiers. The skill of the Huey pilots in getting in and out of tough positions very often meant the difference between life and death for the soldiers on the ground. If a wounded soldier could be evacuated by chopper, he had more chance of surviving.

Left: A member of the 3d Battalion, 60th Infantry Regiment, crosses a stream in February 1967. He is wearing a flak vest over his t-shirt and tied to his back is a sock containing C-ration cans. In his left hand he carries extra ammunition for his squad's M-60 machine gun. He has attached his bayonet to his weapon.

Left: An infantryman is able to enjoy a USO show when out of the field. He is wearing the much loved tropical combat 'boonie' hat. He has personalised it by adding the pull rings from grenades to the camouflage loops around the hat. The 'boonie' hat was made of the same cotton rip stop poplin as the jungle fatigues. Locally manufactured copies could be found made of a wide variety of materials.

Left: A 4th Infantry Division soldier enjoys a hot meal in the field, using his helmet as a stand to support his paper plate. He has subdued rank insignia and name tape on his third pattern jungle jacket.

Below: A radio operator calls in for instructions while his buddy looks on. The radio operator has attached a woven band around his helmet cover for decoration. Such forms of individualisation did not begin to become common until the latter part of the war. The soldier on the right wears a jungle jacket with the subdued U.S. Army tape on the left chest. He does not however have a name tape on the right chest.

An infantry soldier listens in while another soldier radios for support. The soldier on the right has tied two bandoliers around his body to carry magazines for his M-16 rifle, a method of carrying ammunition that became very popular as the war progressed. He is wearing a regular name tape on the right breast of his fatigue jacket. He also appears to have placed issue cellulose tape on the muzzle of his rifle, to keep moisture out of the barrel.

Above: Three members of the 1st Infantry Division take shelter in a shallow hole. The soldier on the left has taken a 1st Infantry Division patch and stuck it behind the helmet's foliage band. He has slung an M-16 bandolier across his chest and attached a smoke grenade to his load bearing equipment. The soldier in the center has stuck a spare magazine in his helmet, and the soldier on the far right has put his helmet on backwards.

Right: An M-60 machine gunner gets ready to move out. He has attached a universal carrying strap to his weapon to act as a sling. He also has attached two canteens to his pistol belt and stuffed the cargo pockets of his trousers. The soldier standing immediately behind him has attached a two-quart collapsible canteen to his equipment.

Left: An M-60 gunner begins to dismantle and clean his squad automatic weapon. He is beginning to clean out some of the dirt in the weapon with a wire brush supplied with the gun.

Left: A soldier prepares to clean his M-16 rifle. He carries bandoliers in lieu of load bearing equipment and has stuffed the pockets of his jungle fatigues. Despite the miserable conditions in which the grunts found themselves, they had to be sure to keep their rifles clean if they were to operate properly when needed.

An M48 A3 tank used by the U.S. Army and USMC armored units in Vietnam. What little armor there was in Vietnam was used to support infantry operations whenever possible. This M48 A3 would have been used for limited off-road operations and to guard convoys etc. The A3 variant can be recognised by its large cupola and the I-R searchlight mounted above the gun mantlet.

Left: Cases of C-rations are delivered by 'mules'. Mules were small utility vehicles that could be used to transport light loads and casualties. Each of the cases stacked on the truck contained 12 meals. Each meal contained a 'main course' and dessert as well as a beverage, heating unit and cigarettes. Also of interest is the 'boonie' hat worn by the man second from the left and the scarf worn by the man second from the right. The scarf appears to be of local manufacture.

Left: Staff Sergeant John Sherrod shaves with his bayonet. The bayonet issued with the M-16 was rarely attached to the rifle and instances of hand to hand combat with the bayonet during the war were few and far between. However, the army continued to issue the bayonet as it had done for hundreds of years and G.I.s continued to find other uses for the bayonet, as they had always done.

Above: Tankers assigned to the Americal Division (a division formed in America and New Caledonia in World War II) work on their M48A3 tank. These men have attached a liberal supply of additional food, rations and other effects designed to make their life more comfortable. They are working to repair damage caused by an enemy rocket.

Right: This man has decided to fight the heat by stripping down to as light a load as possible. He only carries a canteen and extra ammunition for the M-60, and has discarded his fatigue jacket and t-shirt. He has placed an ace of spades card in the foliage band of his helmet as a personal decoration. Items like the card were often used by soldiers as talismans or good luck charms.

Left: First Lieutenant Bob Dean interrogates a Viet Cong prisoner in August 1969. Lieutenant Dean is wearing the Engineer Research and Development Laboratory (ERDL) camouflage that was very popular amongst specialised units in Vietnam. This camouflage was not common amongst the grunts until the final stages of the war. It was constructed to the same specifications as the third pattern utility uniform.

Left: Stanley Ressor, the Secretary of the Army, talks to Private First Class Dominic Martino. Private Martino has chosen not to wear any insignia on his jungle jacket except for his Combat Medics Badge This was awarded to medics who had been directly involved in combat operations with infantry units.

A tunnel rat wearing his M17 gas mask prepares to come out of a Viet Cong tunnel. Gas masks were often worn to clear tunnels to guard against smoke or tear gas. The issue jungle boot can be seen worn over the hole.

Above: The standard rucksack pictured here was manufactured in lightweight nylon and could be worn with or without a tubular metal frame. Folded up just above his rucksack is this soldier's waterproof poncho.

Left: An M-60 gunner is helped in carrying his ammunition by his assistant. The strain of the weight of the gun can be seen on the face of the gunner. Dangling between his legs can be seen a holster for a M1911 .45 caliber automatic pistol. The gunner's assistant is also straightening out a belt of ammunition so that it can be fired without jamming the gun.

Right: Two members of the Americal Division display a communist flag trophy in 1970. Both men are wearing the tropical 'boonie' hat favored by soldiers during the later stages of the war. The men are standing in front of a series of bunkers constructed of sand-bags and ammunition crates.

Right: Two radio operators deliver a message on their standard issue AN/PRC 25 FM set. The soldier on the left has fashioned a scarf by cutting down the issue towel, which he wears with the OG107 t-shirt. The soldier on the right has cut down his t-shirt. He wears issue 'Protective Glasses', which would have been fitted with the individual soldier's prescription. Long hair, like this soldier's, would not have been seen until the latter stages of the war.

Above: Two grunts of the 198th Infantry Brigade struggle to emerge from a rice paddy. The radio man in the front has attached a two-quart canteen, smoke grenade, machete and box of C-rations to the frame carrying his radio. Just visible on his left hip is a claymore carrying bag. These disposable bags were designed to carry two claymore anti-personnel mines, but often were retained to carry additional belongings.

Left: This soldier has weighed himself down with a great deal of extra equipment. Among the items that he has attached to his pack are two issue socks filled with C-ration cans, a civilian bag containing personal items, additional ammunition pouches and an entrenching tool, all of which he wears over his flak jacket. Loads such as this were not uncommon amongst grunts on long operations.

Above: At the end of a patrol, four grunts prepare to board a Huey helicopter to be evacuated. All of the men are traveling light without rucksacks, which would indicate that this was a patrol of short duration. The man on the far right wears a flak jacket with a bandolier draped over his shoulder.

Right: An infantry patrol of the 12th Infantry Regiment returns to Fire Support Base Jamie, typical of support bases throughout the war. The bunkers are constructed from sandbags and pre-fabricated metal siding. Very often, all of the material for a fire support base would simply be packaged together and delivered to the construction site via helicopter.

Private First Class Herman Haynes prepares to report on infantry units taking part in operation
Cedar Falls in January 1967. He is wearing the issue utility cap and third pattern jungle fatigues. He
is using a South Vietnamese Army (ARVN) rucksack favored by many American soldiers to carry
additional belongings. He has tied a poncho to the bottom of his pack and on his left hip he carries
a .45 caliber automatic pistol in its black leather holster.

Above: A grunt takes cover outside a Vietnamese village. He is wearing the lightweight rucksack with an extra canteen attached over the third pattern utility jacket. Slung on his right hip is a claymore bag that appears to contain two claymore mines.

Right: The 25th Infantry Division Arrives in Vung Tau in January 1966. These men all wear OG107 utility uniforms with full color patches. The guidon is ceremonial and would have been kept at the regimental headquarters throughout the division's time in Vietnam. The men are all equipped with M-14 rifles.

Left: During Operation Attleboro in 1966 members of the 1st Battalion, 2nd Infantry Regiment, 1st Infantry Division receive mail. Both of these men are wearing the second pattern utility uniform with concealed buttons and epaulets. The man on the right has a full color US Army tape sewn above the left pocket. The man on the left is wearing a scarf fashioned from parachute material. In his right hand he holds two empty plastic canteens and an open C-ration can.

Below: Members of the 1st Infantry Division check a road for mines. All three men are wearing the M1952 utility armor. The mine detection operator has his gas mask bag attached to his left thigh in the regulation manner. He has also attached a sock full of C-rations to the left epaulet of his flak jacket.

A member of the 4th Infantry Division takes a breather during Operation Paul Revere. The soldier is using the seldom seen 'sleeping gear' carrier of the M1956 equipment set. More often the poncho and other sleeping gear were tied to the frame of the lightweight rucksack.

Left: First Lieutenant Edward Christianson of the 16th Infantry, 1st Infantry Division, calls in for orders during Operation Junction City in May 1967. The handset for the lieutenant's radio has been wrapped in a plastic bag in an effort to keep the moisture out of the mouthpiece of the radio. Christianson also has a compass located in the pouch on his left shoulder.

Left: Sergeant David Flinchum of the 22nd Mechanized Infantry, 4th Infantry Division, reads a book from home. Sergeant Flinchum is wearing the M1952 flak armor; the later model flak jacket featured a standing collar that was designed to protect the neck. Sergeant Flinchum's membership of a mechanized infantry unit explains his use of body armor. Generally, soldiers who spent most of their time on foot did not bother to wear the flak armor.

Right: A soldier warms a can of C-rations using a portable stove. This portable gasoline stove was generally found on vehicles or in stationary positions and was unchanged from World War II. It did provide a change from more commonly used sterno fuel tablets which were said to give an unpalatable taste to food. The chef is wearing OG107 utilities with the white name tape.

Right: A 16th Infantry Regiment member catches his breath during Operation Junction City in February 1967. He has attached a plastic compass pouch to the left shoulder of his load bearing equipment. The canvas M1956 compass/first aid pouch was more frequently seen. Just visible on his left shoulder is the 1st Infantry Division Patch. Patches were not commonly seen being worn by men in the field.

Above: A soldier fires a Colt Automatic Rifle (CAR) 15. The CAR 15 was a lightweight variant of the M-16 that was designed to be carried by officers and soldiers with specialized tasks requiring a lighter weapon. Features of the CAR 15 were a telescopic stock and larger flash suppressor. The CAR 15 was also extensively used by reconnaissance and special forces units.

Below: An M-60 fires on enemy positions. The M-60 was the standard squad automatic weapon of the American soldier in Vietnam. The links that held together the belts of ammunition for the M-60, clearly visible here, would break apart after a round had been fired. The machine gunner has also stuck a spare round for his M-60 into the foliage band of his helmet.

Above: A sniper takes aim with an M1 Garand mounted with a telescopic sight and removable bipod rest. The use of Garands as sniper rifles was not common; the more typical sniper rifle was a modified M-14 rifle. The rest could quickly be removed from the muzzle of the rifle and was also used with the M-14.

Right: Captain Walter Swan signals in for a chopper. Captain Swan has a collapsible two-quart canteen hanging underneath his binoculars. Hanging over his right shoulder can be seen the hollow end of a CAR 15's telescopic stock. Junior officers fought and lived under the same conditions as the men. The lightweight rucksack just visible on the captain's back is as full as those of his men. He wears privately purchased sunglasses to shield his eyes from the sun.

Left: A soldier on water detail prepares to fill his squad's one-quart plastic canteens. Grunts usually carried at least two canteens with them on an operation, often more. This man also wears an unusual combination of a either a first or second pattern jungle fatigue jacket, identifiable by the adjustable tab at the waist and OG107 utility trousers, identifiable by the patch pockets. The jungle fatigues and utilities were not often worn together.

Right: A soldier in OG107 utilities crosses a river carrying cases of C-rations. While he is not wearing any equipment, he is carrying his M-16 which would indicate that he is in an area close to the enemy.

During an operation in September 1966, two members of the 9th Infantry Regiment, 25th Infantry Division, pass through a stream. The man at the front is wearing the second pattern jungle fatigue jacket with concealed buttons and epaulets. Also of interest are the glasses being worn by the man following behind him. These are issue glasses, which would have been fitted with the soldier's prescription.

Above: A 1st Cavalry Division helicopter delivers food and beverages to soldiers at a forward position in October 1966. The helicopter crewman is wearing a subdued 1st Cavalry Division patch on his fatigue uniform. He is also wearing a locally procured black baseball hat. Among the supplies being offloaded from the helicopter is a cooler, seen here on the ground next to the three water cans. The cooler could be used to deliver either hot or cold food to the troops.

Opposite page, top: Water buffaloes observe grunts searching through their village. The soldier at the front has clipped his compass to the front of his nylon load bearing equipment suspenders. More practical in the field, the new pattern nylon components (designated M1967)

were never available in quantities large enough to be issued as complete sets, but were instead worn in conjunction with the canvas gear. The man has also taped green electrical tape to his M-16 to help camouflage it.

Opposite page, bottom: A squad of infantrymen are carried into battle on the top of a M113 Armored Personnel Carrier. Soldiers would often travel on the outside of vehicles so they could easily and quickly dismount. All of the infantrymen have draped themselves with spare ammunition for their squad's M-60 machine gun. The man seated on the left has pinned a button to the outside of his helmet and has draped an olive green towel around his neck to fight moisture.

Left: A member of the 28th Infantry Regiment rests, using his entrenching tool as a stool. He has draped a rope around himself and just visible on his left side is a claymore bag. Attached to the back of his load bearing equipment are a smoke grenade and two canteens.

Left: Captain Michael Quealy performs religious services for 1st Infantry Division members. Quealy's congregation is wearing a variety of fatigue uniforms and some of them have draped white towels around their necks. This would have been unusual in the field, with the olive green towels being far more prevalent.

Right: Major General William Depuy discusses the course of Operation Battle Creek with one of his officers in November 1966. General Depuy wears a rain coat over his first pattern jungle uniform. Depuy has subdued name tapes sewn to the front of his jungle uniform and has his rank embroidered in black on the front of his helmet. Such modifications to helmet covers would have been done locally.

Right: A grunt leaning up against a tree branch to catch his breath. This soldier is typical of thousands of others. He has chosen not to wear any body armor or under-shirt in order to fight the heat. On the elastic band around his helmet this man has written his name as a further means of identification.

Left: Captain Vickery has just been awarded a silver star and poses for his official picture. He is wearing a first pattern OG107 utility jacket. His jacket is fully 'badged' and features a variety of full color insignia – jackets like this would have been worn in rear areas. Underneath his jacket, Vickery is wearing a white t-shirt. On his left shoulder is the red and yellow insignia of the 25th Infantry Division. Over the black and gold U.S. Army name tape Vickery wears an embroidered pair of jump wings and combat infantry badge. Over his white name tape he wears Vietnamese jump wings.

Below: Members of the 4th Infantry Division board the *General Pope* in July 1966 for shipment to Vietnam. These men are shipping overseas in full combat gear. They are wearing the OG107 utility uniform and black leather combat boots. These would have been exchanged for more appropriate jungle fatigues and boots upon arrival in Vietnam. The lightweight rucksack being carried by the man at the rear of the column illustrates how the pack was worn when full, as well as showing the frame on which the pack was carried.

Right: A flame thrower operator from the 25th Infantry Division rests under the weight of his weapon. In addition to his flame thrower, this man also carries an M-16 rifle. He has discarded his shirt and only wears the M1952 flak jacket. The weight of the flame thrower precluded it from being carried on patrols or long operations.

Below: A member of the 25th Infantry Division guards suspected Viet Cong prisoners. He is wearing black leather field boots and the OG107 utility shirt with jungle fatigue pants. His jacket has its full array of insignia. The insignia includes a red and yellow full color divisional patch on the left shoulder, black and yellow U.S. Army tape on the left chest and white name tape on the right chest. This might indicate that the picture was taken prior to 1966, but although subdued insignia was officially required as of January 1967, supply and availability problems meant that both full color and mixtures of subdued and full color insignia continued to be worn for some time after this date. Indeed, some elite units such as the 101st Airborne Division retained their full color patches throughout the conflict.

Opposite page, top: Three men deliver emergency first aid to a wounded comrade. All three of the men are wearing their flak armor. The two men kneeling at the front of the picture have the M1956 combat field pack 'butt' pack attached to their equipment. This pack was found to be unsatisfactory in the field and was frequently replaced by the lightweight rucksack. The man on the right also carries an M1911 .45 automatic pistol in a shoulder harness.

Opposite page, bottom: Four men discuss the day's activities. The man seated on the right has fashioned a headband out of t-shirt material to help keep sweat out of his eyes.

The soldier in front of him has draped a towel around his shoulders to wipe sweat from his face. He also wears the popular 'boonie' hat. The two men standing have also taken measures to fight the heat. The man on the far left has rolled up the legs of his trousers, affording a good view of the height of the jungle boots.

Above: A patrol sets out. The man at the rear has draped a two-quart collapsible canteen over his M1956 load bearing equipment, in addition to the one-quart canteen attached to his right hip. He is wearing a locally manufactured camouflaged 'boonie' hat.

Above: Two members of the 25th Infantry Division return fire during operations around Cu Chi in May 1966. The man on the right is wearing OG107 utility trousers, a t-shirt and the M1952 flak jacket. The picture gives a good view of the side lacing on the jacket which was used to help adjust the size of the vest.

Left: A sergeant in the 25th Division crosses a stream. He is wearing a utility jacket with full color insignia, including yellow and green sergeant's stripes on his sleeves. He has attached a smoke grenade to his equipment. Floating on his left side is a claymore bag. The fact that it is floating would indicate that he is using the bag to carry personal gear and not the two claymore mines that came in the bag

Soldiers in a stationary position sit around their M-60 machine gun, which has been mounted on an older .30 caliber tripod mount. These mounts greatly added to the weapon's effectiveness, but their additional weight precluded much use in the field. Ammunition cans for the gun are visible just underneath the M-60.

Left: Immediate fire support for infantrymen was often provided by mortars like the 80mm pictured here. The gunner on the right wears a badged utility shirt. Interestingly, he has pinned a metal version of the combat infantry badge to his shirt. On utility uniforms the combat infantry badge was usually an embroidered patch sewn to the shirt.

Left: Three men wearing OG107 utilities with jungle boots use a tunnel exploration kit to search an enemy tunnel. These kits were rare and did not reach Vietnam in significant numbers until almost the end of American involvement in Vietnam. The kit consisted of a light that could be attached to the head. The round container on the right side of the center man contained telephone wire. He is armed with a .38 pistol equipped with a silencer.

Heavily laden grunts prepare to move out. The man looking over his right shoulder has secured a can of ammunition to the top of his lightweight rucksack. He is wearing first pattern utility trousers with exposed buttons on the thigh pockets. He is leaning forward to offset the weight of his pack.

Left: Soldiers unload supplies from a Huey helicopter. The men are wearing a combination of utility uniforms and jungle fatigues.

Left: Members of the 4th Infantry Division receive a hot meal in the field, which would have been delivered by helicopter. The food is being served out of coolers and placed on metal trays. A hot meal such as this would have been considered a luxurious change from C-rations. The men are wearing a combination of jackets and t-shirts. The man standing second from the left has a t-shirt that has stretched out of shape due to the humidity experienced during operations in the field.

Above: The 28th Infantry Regiment arrives in Vietnam in October 1965. The men are all wearing OG107 utilities with full color insignia. The bayonet for their M-14 rifle is attached to the entrenching tool cover. The streamers hanging from the flag on the right are battle honors awarded to the Regiment since its founding in the 19th century. Such a neat and uniform appearance would have quickly become more individualised once these men got into the field.

Right: An M26 fragmentation grenade has been wired to a post for a simple booby trap. The M26 was the standard fragmentation grenade of the U.S. soldier in Vietnam. These would be carried secured to straps on the side of the ammunition pouch, or carried in a variety of other ways.

Left: An M-60 gunner and his assistant try to advance rapidly under the weight of their weapons and equipment. In addition to his machine gun and ammunition, the machine gunner at the front is hindered by a full set of M1956 web gear as well as the gas mask carrying bag attached to his left hip.

Left: A 4th Infantry Division soldier takes a breather. He has bloused his trousers into the canvas and leather jungle combat boot. This boot was a great improvement over the earlier all-leather service boot. He has attached several M26 grenades to his ammunition pouches. The M1956 ammunition pouches contained straps that were designed specifically to carry grenades in this manner. He has also taped together two magazines for his M-16 to ensure rapid reloading.

Right: A medic treats a wounded soldier of the 9th Infantry Division. The wounded man is wearing the utility uniform while the medic is wearing the jungle utilities. The medic's bag is open in the center of the picture.

Right: Members of the 60th Infantry Regiment, 9th Infantry Division cross a stream while on an operation in 1967. The man at the front is wearing the first pattern grenade vest, which was designed to carry individual rounds for the M79 grenade launcher. Later versions were made from nylon and nylon mesh. The man holds the grenade launcher in his left hand to keep it out of the water. The grenadier has secured a number of items to his helmet underneath the elastic band.

Opposite page, top: A UH1 Huey prepares to deliver a load of infantrymen into a landing zone (LZ). The Huey was the workhorse of the Vietnam war and perhaps the Army's most famous helicopter. It could carry 11 infantryman into or out of an engagement. The Huey was also used to transport supplies and evacuate wounded.

Opposite page, bottom: A CH-47 Chinook helicopter unloads its cargo of infantryman. The Chinook was a larger cargo helicopter that could transport as many as 30 fully equipped men to the field. It could also be used to deliver supplies and light artillery.

Above: Members of the 60th Infantry, 9th Infantry Division, search a hedge for enemy soldiers. The man on the left has secured his cigarettes to the elastic band of his camouflage helmet cover.

Right: A soldier of the 11th Infantry Regiment, 5th Infantry Division, cleans his weapon immediately after returning from an operation. His lightweight rucksack and his other equipment is around him. Also visible is the suspension system for his helmet liner, which consisted of olive green webbing that could be adjusted to any head size.

Left: An M-60 gunner of the 11th Infantry, 5th Infantry Division, enjoys a cigarette. He is holding his flak armor in his right hand. He has draped extra ammunition for his M-60 over his lightweight rucksack. He has also unbloused his trousers to increase ventilation.

Left: An infantryman wearing ERDL camouflage utility uniform enjoys the scenery from inside a UH1 Huey. This camouflage was not widely worn by Army infantrymen during the war, but was very popular with reconnaissance and special forces units. He is wearing a very individualised 'boonie' hat that is being held in place by securing the chin strap to the back of the head. To his right can be seen the back of the second pattern M69 vest.

Right: Two members of the 101st feed their pet. These men show two different methods of personalising their 'boonie' hats. Also of interest are the full color 101st Airborne patches being worn with subdued name tapes. The 101st Airborne never adopted a subdued version of their insignia.

This M113 is helping these soldiers keep their feet dry. All of these men are wearing flak jackets. The second man on the left is a crew member of the vehicle who is wearing a standard helmet, while the vehicle commander, third from the left, wears the combat vehicle crew helmet.

Two members of the 173rd Airborne Brigade – widely known as 'The Herd' during their long tour of duty in Vietnam – show off a lawn mower donated by the citizens of Englewood, Florida, to allow the men to clear their positions. The soldier on the left wears the first pattern fatigue uniform with exposed buttons. The man on the right wears the OG107 utilities with full color insignia and black web waist belt. The 173rd was the only Airborne Brigade to stay fully jump qualified throughout its time in Vietnam.

MSG Thomas Kinsman poses for a photograph after receiving his medal of honor. Kinsman is wearing the green wool service uniform. The lanyard on his right shoulder is light blue for infantry and the disks on his collar also denote his branch of service.

Above: Returnees from Vietnam receive their new green service jackets. All of them are wearing the khaki cotton service uniform that they would have been wearing when they left Vietnam. The man on the right is wearing his field jacket for extra warmth. The service jackets have the insignia for U.S. Army, Vietnam. Note the members of the 101st Airborne Division, identifiable by their jump wings, distinctive crests, garrison caps and trousers bloused over their coveted jump boots.

Below: In Tacoma, Washington 1967, returning members of the 101st Airborne Division receive local information and advice from other soldiers. When a patch was worn on the right shoulder it was called the battle patch.